European Brain Snakes

European Brain Snakes

Snakes

In Which We Surmise that the Brain Is

Ireland and We Call for St. Patrick

Douglas Wilson

canonpress
Moscow, Idaho

Table of Contents

Preamble

And the Frankish magi and sayers of sooth approached the emperor, and said not to be afraid of this serpent of YHWH. For the word and rod of the wise man had become a great serpent before the emperor. "Lo," they said, "do we not have brain snakes every bit as large as this one?" And they published their snakes in a refereed journal. But the serpent of the wise man came unto the brain snakes, and swallowed them up. And thus it was that the brain snakes became tummy snakes (Ex. 7:8-13).

These things are a parable, line on line, precept on precept.

CHAPTER 1

Seeping Postmodernism

For many reasons, none of them intellectually compelling, postmodern thinking proper, along with postmodern assumptions unacknowledged, are making great headway in the "post-conservative" evangelical world. One lesson that we can take from the postmodernist playbook in this regard is that fooling around with language is actually a disguised power grab. While denying their point (because they always privilege their own discourse), I do want to turn it on them. Their fundamental dishonesty in reasoning and refusal to deal with God as He has revealed Himself, can only signal the presence of that old adversary in the camp, which is, of course, *unbelief.* These are not mere differences of opinion, or denominational distinctives.

This lie (for that is what it is) cloaks itself in "epistemic humility" and postures for the cameras, all the while telling us that this demeanor of theirs is the foundation of *authentic* evangelism. In other words, living in community "with authenticity" is apparently to be built on the philosophical foundation of denying that there is any such a thing as authenticity.

This postmodern foolishness (that is seeping in among us and is now puddling around our shoes) should not be treated by us as an invitation to dialog. We are not being summoned to cordial discourse between various local faith communities, with the faith once delivered being treated as though it is nothing more than the grammar of our particular community. I am reminded of a comment that the great Southern Presbyterian theologian J.H. Thornwell made about his colleague from Kentucky, the great Robert Breckenridge. "What he does, he does with his might. Where he loves, he loves with his whole soul; when he hates, he hates with equal cordiality; and when he fights, he wants a clear field and nothing to do but fight." When it comes to this pomo stuff, it would take about two cents to get me into a Breckenridge mode.

A similar taunt of defiance was written by C.S. Lewis in his classic *That Hideous Strength*. Speaking of the "fabulously learned and saintly Richard Crowe" he notes that the last words of Crowe had been "Marry, Sirs, if Merlin who was the Devil's son was a true King's man as ever ate bread, is it not a shame that you, being but the sons of bitches, must be rebels and regicides?" Sons of bitches about pegs it.

I use these words deliberately, because it reveals how much postmodern thinking has penetrated the evangelical world. I am not here speaking of those writers who are openly cheering postmodernism and throwing their hats in the air. I am speaking of churches and individual Christians who flinch and wince at the free use of "sons of bitches" and who do not wince at all when someone says that "objective truth" may be a concept that will not serve us well evangelistically in these postmodern times. "Jesus is Lord" is a truth, to be sure, but it is a truth in *our* linguistic community. And the compromised say that they may not agree with this, but surely we can conduct our discourse on a higher level?

At the end of the day, any theologian who defends the truth as an objective reality apart from our experience of it will be charged with epistemic arrogance and hubris. This charge will be made regardless of his personal demeanor, grace, or graciousness. This charge will be made because the use of language in this debate is all about who will "have the center." The pomos want it, and they will lie to get it.

And so you see the real offense of the "serrated edge." The serrated edge does not just indicate a willingness to stand for the truth that Jesus is Lord outside all "linguistic communities," that He is the Lord of heaven and earth. It does show this, but it reveals much more. The use of the serrated edge shows that we *anticipate* the charge of hubris, arrogance, and all the rest of it, and we don't care. It shows that we know we are in a fight— which cannot be said of many evangelicals who do not yet realize how fundamentally they have been compromised by the spirit of the age. Who gives greater offense to the evangelical by-stander on the sidelines? The one who says that authentic Christianity has to give up its claims to absolute truth to remain authentic? Or the one who said "sons of bitches"? Pietism is not just confused, it is impotent—and resents being told that.

This is why a favored tactic that is used to advance the postmodern agenda is an adroit use of "demands for an apology." I have noticed that many Christians would be suspicious if someone simply announced that the lines between right and wrong, good and evil, truth and falsehood, need to be blurred. Believing Christians hear something like this, and say, "Wait a minute . . ." Such blurring, therefore, is often advanced in a much more personal (and practical) way. The tactic is effective because believing Christians are often *personally* humble and, while they don't mind defending the truth of the faith, they are much less comfortable about defending themselves. So the postmodern blurrers-of-lines go about it this way.

Here it is in a short form. They make an accusation, wait for the denial, and then offer to split the difference. Take an absurd form of this for purposes of illustration. A godly person is accused of shoplifting at ten area department stores. He denies it, indignantly. The accusers then suggest that he demonstrate his humility by "apologizing" for shoplifting at *one* of them. But of course, he didn't do any shoplifting. If he refuses, he is upbraided for his pride and stubbornness. "Must think he is sinless." If he agrees, for the sake of peace, he has agreed to a lie, and a blurring of the lines between truth and a lie. If he has agreed fundamentally, he has been taken out of the conflict between truth and lies. If he has (sinfully) compromised in it, but still seeks to remain in the battle, then the same drill will be run on him again.

In the realm of faith, apologies (i.e. seeking forgiveness) occur, and they occur all the time. But the truth of God's Word should govern the entire process. If someone has sinned, that person should confess it. If he has not, he should not. Offering an apology simply as a means of making peace (detached from the truth) is an offense against God. Offering an apology to get the adversaries to lay off is capitulation and surrender. The whole thing is a basic *tactic* of theirs, and like so many of their tactics (I wish this were the sixteenth century so that I could use the phrase *knavish tricks* here), the whole thing is knit together with lies.

This is why it is necessary to employ satire, lampooning, and so on, in our response to postmodernism. In Scripture, such tactics are to be employed against Christ-denying Pharisees, statists, apostates, and so on. This is simply another way of affirming what I have always affirmed about the point of lawful satire, which is that it is fundamentally to be aimed at religious arrogance. This is an argument I laid out in *The Serrated Edge*, but the difficulty comes (as always) in the *application*. Stuffed-shirt Pharisees almost never identify *themselves* in this way. "Pharisee" was a term of praise until Jesus got done with it. No one knocks on your door and says, "Hello, I am here as an agent of Hell, and I have come to lead you astray."

In other words, if you ever knock a wolf (in sheep's clothing) a good one, the chances are outstanding that said wolf will start bleating like you are some kind of maniac shepherd. So remember where we are. This is an attack on postmodernists within the evangelical camp, those who are now saying that there is *no such thing as absolute truth*, that there are no metanarratives, not even those revealed by God, and so on. We shouldn't use this kind of language on Baptists for dunking, or Presbyterians for sprinkling, which would evidence a complete lack of proportion.

But postmodernism reeks like a sulfur pit, and if I ever stop throwing rocks at this hellish Apparition from the Academy, it is only because my arm is tired. Postmodernism, in the forms I am attacking, *is* apostasy. That is the point.

Do we run the risk of confusing our own applications of scriptural principles with Scripture itself? That is of course a possible temptation. But it does not follow from this that no applications can be made with scriptural authority. We are *required* in Scripture to make such applications with scriptural authority. If we do not have the capacity to draw on Scripture as we teach Christians how to paint, compose, vote, dance, sing, write, and so on, then this would not be *Christian* cultural leadership at all. But if it *is* Christian cultural leadership, then there are applications we must be making from Scripture. We do not look at Christians who differ with us in order to say that "your guess is as good as mine."

There must be a way of saying that the *reveling* that St. Paul prohibited in the New Testament corresponds to a 21st century *rave*. Without such applications, the Scriptures are sufficient for nothing other than being admired from afar. No situation that any of us have faced in the course of our lives is *exactly* parallel to the particular issues addressed in the Bible.

In short, it is an *applied* Bible that is sufficient. Put another way, the Bible alone is sufficient for *all applications.* The Bible does not step in for us and make the applications itself. And if the Bible is not applied by us to situations it never mentions by name, then how could it be sufficient? Sufficient for what? There are many answers to the question, but smacking postmodernism is one of them.

All Christians are called to preserve the unity of the Spirit in the bond of peace. But before we charge off to do this, we need to distinguish between catholicity and mush. A catholic or ecumenical spirit is not an optional add-on extra. But there is a vast difference between Christians who love each other in Christ, despite various doctrinal differences (known and acknowledged), and a "lower common denominator" unity which has been a modern evangelical specialty for a generation or so. This problem has grown considerably as the "denominator" has gradually broadened, and now takes in all sorts of "communities of faith." And this has been heightened in the last few years as postmodernist evangelicals (an oxymoron, by the way) have taken this dictum, called, and raised it ten. In *A New Kind of Christian*, Brian McLaren now addresses the problems of ecumenicity across different *faiths*, and not just different denominations of trinitarian Christians. He deals with this issue by saying that it is none of our business who goes to Heaven and who goes to Hell. Besides being an obvious dodge, it invites the next obvious question—is it any of our business if there *is* a Heaven or Hell?

J. Gresham Machen was right in his classic book *Christianity and Liberalism*. Liberalism was not a variant of the Christian faith, it was another faith altogether. The liberalism of Machen's day constituted nothing more or less than simple unbelief. The same thing is true of postmodernism in our day. It is nothing but unbelief, and unbelief and orthodoxy mix about as well as kerosene and sherry. This may be dismissed by some as "irascibility," but there it is. Someone will ask if I am willing to drop the H-bomb—is postmodernism heresy? *Of course it is*. It is another religion, and other religions decked out in Christian garb is what genuine heresy actually is.

And this is one of the central problems that I have had with the sectarians of the Reformed world—those "Truly-Reformeds" (TRs) who glibly use the epithet *heresy* to describe *denominational* differences. Having been on the receiving end of that treatment, I am loathe to do unto others what has been done unto me. It is unbiblical for one thing, and stupid for another. And one of the reasons it is stupid is that the Christian faith is facing a momentous challenge in postmodernism, which is another worldview and faith altogether. And *this* is the moment that some have chosen to declare war on fellow Christians for bringing children under the age of eight to the Lord's Table. They are not fighting heresy—they are actually *refusing* to. In the meantime, postmodern mush masquerading as catholicity is rampant in the broader Church.

Why Lies Digest Well

As Flannery O'Connor once put it, "The truth does not change according to our ability to stomach it." But a falsehood, as Chesterton notes, is engineered precisely so that the listeners would in fact be able to stomach it. *Stomachability* is a design feature when it comes to a lie. Who would invent lies that nobody is going to want to believe?

But the truth simply is what it is.

This is why truth tellers are so consistently troublemakers. And this is also why the postmodern heart loves the coherence view of truth, and detests the correspondence view of truth. The coherence view includes all those things that might be pleasant to digest, and the correspondence view encompasses the rest of the world, which is not really all that edible. It is measured by criteria other than how it might make us feel half an hour after dinner.

This is why, incidentally, C.S. Lewis is beloved by conservative American evangelicals even though he wasn't one of us. He hated subjectivism, and saw that subjectivism was the portal through which every foul error is able to make its way into the lives of believers. It is the same portal, come to think of it, from which Rob Bell made his escape. The world is simply *there*, and we are the ones who must conform to it, and not the other way around.

When we conform to the world we are doing with natural revelation what God has trained us to do with special revelation. The issue for us must be "what does the Bible say?" and not "what would we like the Bible to have said?" We learn to read the world because we have been trained by the primer of the Word, and the very first lesson we must learn in order to become "men with chests" is that the right kind of sentiment rests upon an objective moral code that will not budge, however much we wheedle and whine about it.

So here is a postmodern math problem, a story problem, for the current crop of Mark Studdocks that the government school system is busy right now shaping into that shapeless . . . you know what I mean. "There are ten redwoods on the mountainside. Loggers have come with a permit and have cut three of them down. How does this make you feel?"

This postmodern goo thought is capable of seeping into all kinds of surprising places. I have seen it get to places that at one time I would have said were entirely inaccessible. But denominational walls cannot keep it out. Institutions cannot save themselves with little pieces of paper called founding documents. The only thing that can spare us is truth defended at the testing point, which is to say, the need of the hour is courage.

CHAPTER 3
Painting the Couch

I rise in praise of propositions, but not the propositions of bad philosophers who try to reify everything they touch. Rather, I praise the propositions of the competent and godly English teacher, and, although this is not the point of our current discussion, I also praise clauses, imperatives, nouns, verbs, alphabets, jots and tittles.

A proposition is simply a statement of fact, and the fact that God allows us to see things in the world, and transfer what we see into the minds of others by this means, is simply a grand mystery and miracle, right up there with the loaves and fishes. Here I am, sitting with my laptop, listening to the blues, and depositing thoughts into your head. How does *that* work? This does not explain things fully, but one of the necessary instruments involved in all this is the lowly proposition. *The green armadillo dances on our coffee table.* See? Not only can propositions point to the real world, they are also the building blocks of the glorious world of fiction—and *there*, the relationship of the proposition to the world God made is far more glorious and subtle.

I have been attacking the arbitrary and idolatrous absolutism of the Enlightenment for years. But their problem is that they attributed absolutes to their Baal, and not that they attributed absolutes to anyone. And when Elijah opposed them, it was truth claim against truth claim, proposition against proposition. Baal is god. Yahweh is God. Which will it be? And Elijah did not simply oppose duddy truth claim to duddy truth claim; *his* truth claim was kind of on fire.

False absolutes are not a post-Enlightenment development. The Pharisees searched the Scriptures because they thought that in them they would find eternal life. But the words they were looking *at* bore actual testimony to Jesus, the one they were rejecting. This way of slipping off the point is as old as dirt, and though modernity and postmodernity are both guilty of it in different ways, the problem did not enter the world with post-Cartesian developments.

Propositions, received in simple faith, by simple people who don't over-engineer things, are windows *through which* we see. They are not murals *at which* we stare. The modernist philosophers want to make propositions into murals. The postmodernists want to maintain (rightly, so far as it goes) that if all we are going to do is stare at the painted window as though it were a wall, we might as well paint over the mural with whatever colors are currently gripping us, or go off to look at some other part of the wall. But the point is to look *through* the propositions—at Jesus, the author and finisher of our faith. I am not going to abandon my propositional window just because some other guy with a philosophical bent got paint all over his.

So there it is. I am not about to give up propositions, and the reason I will not is because Jesus meets me there. He meets me in the words, the sentences, the commands, the questions, and the propositions—provided I read and listen like a Christian.

We can look at the Lord's Supper to illustrate the point. Christ meets us there for blessing when we assemble in faith. But if we gather around His table to debate the flour, or the grapes, or the tablecloth, or the metaphysics, we are trying to meet the Lord by coming *at* the Table. We are trying to wrest control of it from Him, which is folly. We are rather called to come *through* the Table. It is a *means* of grace. The idolater who comes is stopped short. The one who comes in evangelical faith comes through.

It is the same with the words of God, and our words in response. Words are what they are because Jesus is the Word. This means that Jesus is the Poem, He is the Noun, He is the everlasting Verb. Jesus is the Metaphor; He is God and He is with God at the same time. Jesus is the Proposition of God. I am not going to abandon my propositions; they are a gift of God. How could I abandon them? I worship a Proposition. And I defy anyone to turn this into some truncated and dry propositional*ism*, because I worship a Story and a Poem also. I am a Christian. That means I am as logocentric as it gets.

One of the most exasperating features of emergent church thinking is the constant tendency to set propositional statements over against narrative. Abandoning propositions, they are trying to recover the idea of pastor as story-teller. As I have pointed out before, this is like abandoning verbs and nouns in favor of sentences, or ditching lumber for the sake of houses. Stories are made up of propositions. "In a castle by a lake lived a little boy with his green dragon" is proposition. "Jesus rose from the dead" is a proposition.

This confusion is so widespread, and yet so simplistic, it is worth asking what on earth the emergent folks are *reacting* to. For it must be a reaction and clearly does not represent a well-thought out position. When they reject propositional theology in favor of story, what do they *think* they are rejecting? I believe the problem they have with "propositions" is caused by the fact that ministers do not act like they believe their propositions (whether they are found in dogmatic theology, may its tribe increase, or in stories). This problem is actually as old as dirt too, and the reaction to it does not deserve to be dignified with a breathless, cutting edge term like *post*-modernism. When Jesus came along and began teaching with authority, and not as the scribes, the twelve disciples did not begin identifying themselves as post-scribal. What the postmodernists and emergent church johnnies are reacting to is the perennial problem of ecclesiastics who have positional authority without having what we call moral authority. But moral authority is granted by the Spirit of God, and not by spastic reactions to the dull guys who are currently in charge. It takes more than just quitting your job as pastor in the ho-hum church and starting up a new "emergent" church in a nightclub to obtain moral authority. Where is the improvement if we move from dull people doing normal things to dull people doing weird things?

If your living room is dull, nothing changes just because you rearrange the furniture. Of course, if you get really exasperated with the Dullness, you can liven things up for about fifteen minutes if you paint the couch with orange latex. But after that, it is *still* a dull place to be, and the couch is sticky.

The rabbis who did not have the authority that Jesus had could not have remedied their problem by getting an eyebrow pierced. Okay, a bit of excitement for a sabbath or two, but when we all settle down again, he *still* preaches like dishwater left in the sink overnight. And if he goes for another three weeks and tries to regain the previous excitement by getting the other eyebrow pierced, you have a good picture of the vanity of the emergent church. Ironmongery and sticky couches will never give you something to say. And if you have nothing to say, that fact will always be evident to everyone shortly.

Propositions are among the most thrilling gifts that God ever gave to us. But sin blinds us, and those who cannot see this are spiritual dullards. This includes people who professionally handle their dusty books propositions in the Ssshhh! Library of God, as well as those who pretend to throw propositions away in order to tell us all a Really Exciting Metanarrative. But for starters, exciting metanarratives don't have words like metanarrative in the title. In Anglo/Saxon, this word would be rendered as Bigstory, or in western parlance, Tall Tale. As they reject propositions, I await the results with the same anticipation of a customer in a diner who has ordered an omelet from a cook who doesn't believe in eggs anymore. In either case, all who treat propositions with contempt are spiritual dullards—and whether they are scribes or post-scribes doesn't much matter.

Emergent advocates consistently oppose the importance of "story" to the land of arid "propositions," whence they are departing. I have been arguing that this is simply a profound category confusion—stories are made of propositions, emergents argue in their theological works for the importance of story by means of propositions, and so on. So whatever it is they are doing, it is *not* abandoning propositions. Rather, what they are doing is rejecting one story in favor of another, and the story they are telling is that they are departing from the land of darkness, where there are no stories. This is simply false.

As an aside, I am aware of those modern-day Platonists who want to argue for the ontological existence of propositions up in Euclidville, and who want to understand these heavenly propositions in a way detached from dirt, grass, oil and other manifestations of concrete particularity. They want their pristine Ps and Qs, and little invisible hoses running from the heavens down into our sentences to impart to those earthly sentences whatever meaning they might come to possess. I am not interacting with them directly here because I stopped paying any attention to them many years ago.

When I say something like "propositions rock," I am exhibiting no indebtedness whatever to these analytic people who have Hellenism wrapped tight around their axle. Rather, in full Hebraic mode, I am exulting in the fact that "Hear O Israel, the Lord our God is one Lord" concludes with a rousing proposition, and "Jesus is Lord" is *entirely* propositional, even when written in

Greek. A proposition is true or false to the extent that it is being true (or not) to the world the way God made it.

Now, do propositions *exist*? Sure, they exist for the same reason that my English muffins for breakfast used to exist. Propositions, like muffins, are events in the world. I ate my muffins, and I just now wrote the proposition that "the grass on my front lawn is green." Now Plato would want some sort of ontological super-proposition in the sky (and that's what *he* would call "existing"). But I don't pay attention to him because he wanted a giant muffin in the sky too.

Incarnational propositions, street propositions, rough and tumble propositions do not exist off in some autonomous spiritual zone. They fill up our sentences, hymn books, Bibles, prayer books, not to mention books of emergent whining. They are events in the world. The propositional events in the world that are true are those which conform to creation as God gave it. Those that are false do not conform to God's Word.

When we go this way, life is simple. I want to think the way God wants me to think, and this means thinking His thoughts after Him. And if He reveals to us things like "Jesus is Lord," along with "Jesus entered Capernaum," one of the first duties of Christian discipleship is to throw up our hands in the air and shout, "Yay! Some true propositions! Let's believe them!"

Now let us bring this back to the foolish emergent juxtaposition of "story" and "propositions." Just as propositions are inescapable, *so are stories.* The emergents and pomos have their story. The modernists have their story. The Christians have their story. Our propositions are at war with the propositions of the other teams, and our stories are at war with them as well. It is simply false to assume that the modernists are "story-less." They have a *compelling* story. They have a big bang story of creation, they have the story of Darwinian evolution, they have the story of slavery in the Egypt of medieval superstitions, they have Moses bringing in the Enlightenment, they have the story of how religion creates nothing but one Thirty Years War after another, and so on. Now in the last several generations their story has gotten threadbare, and they have grown weary (and vulnerable) in the telling of it. And the pomos are trying to mount a challenge and offer an alternative story, but it is one that cannot be successful because of all the internal contradictions and confusions.

Christians have a story (chock full of propositions, and true ones to boot) that genuinely mounts a challenge to the dominant modernist story. Now we in the confessional Christian church have sinned, but not because we have no story. Rather we have sinned because we have told that story in a dull and lackluster way. We have spoken without authority, just like the scribes. There is a vast difference between a story badly told, and no story at all. The modernists had a story that beguiled the western world for several centuries, but they also have fallen off their game, and have begun to tell it in a tired way. The emergent advocates (with their postmodernism lite) think to take advantage of the opportunity by telling us all an incoherent story, filled with piffle. So the fact that pomos and emergents are taking shots at the modernists is not an encouragement. I feel about it the same way I feel about Dwarves shooting arrows at Calormen.

And so this is the real issue—spiritual authority. The one who tells the story right, wins. The postmodernists see at least this much, but interpret all "winning" as a raw power game. But we serve a God who raises the dead, and the power of the resurrection is not coercive power but resurrection authority bestowed on a servant heart. There is much more to say about this matter of authority, but for the present, Jesus lived and told the story right. And He rose from the dead. And He is Lord. Arid propositions? They wish.

What if someone objects that no one could possibly think that emergent leaders are challenging "statements." Well, if we are talking about statements that are *true*, I do. *They* do, and their books are full of such questioning.

Emergent writers are not primarily reacting to what is going on in analytic philosophy departments. They are revolting against *certainty in pulpits*. In the background is an assumption that the only way preachers could be certain is by borrowing epistemic certainty from the philosophers. Some orthodox apologists influenced by modernity *have* done this, and I would urge them to quit it. But there is another issue, and another source of certainty. The Bible demands that preachers speak the very oracles of God. The pulpit is required to be the place where we hear "thus says the Lord," and not, "it seems to me, at least for now."

The beginning of McLaren's book *A New Kind of Christian* revolves around his rejection of this very point. The pastor in transition is exasperated by certainty in a fellow minister. His whole rejection is of *any kind of* certainty.

And the whole emergent project is not simply saying that this certainty is based on a false and idolatrous foundation, a foundation laid by Descartes, and the way for us to find true certainty is "the following." Rather, the move is to say that because certainty is built on this Cartesian foundation (and it is assumed that this is the only possible foundation that "certainty" could ever have), that therefore our task of ministry in the postmodern world is to urge humility, with that humility understood as some form of principled uncertainty. This is a snare and delusion. It is epistemology straight from the Pit.

Emergent thinking, as such, is simply another form of unbelief, being peddled to us by the ever subtle enemy of our souls. One of the principle qualifications for a minister and Christian shepherd is the ability to detect the presence of wolves. And I am saying that they are here in the sheepfold, right now. Lest I be misunderstood, I am not saying that all those participating in the emergent movement, taken distributively, are wolves. There is a difference between a wolf and a sheep in a wolf's jaws. Every bogus movement in the history of the church has suckered some of the faithful into thinking it is not that big a deal, at least for a time. This happens because wolves are a threat to sheep.

But this particular stew is being cooked up in old Slewfoot's kitchen. I'm not having any, and I am urging all Christians anywhere, all those who love Jesus, to put down their spoons. There is death in the pot.

CHAPTER 4

A Quest for My Feet

One time I was manfully working through *The Next Reformation* by Carl Raschke. In the course of my reading, I came across this. "The philosophical quest for unfailing presuppositions is not Christian; it is *outright paganism*" (p. 113, emphasis his).

But presuppositions are not something you go off and hunt for, like the Holy Grail. Presuppositions are not something you "don't have" until you find some. Presuppositions are only acknowledged or unacknowledged, coherent or incoherent. They are always present. You have never had a conversation with a man who did not have all his presuppositions banging away on all eight cylinders. Raschke is trying to tell us a story of the man who went off hiking on a quest to find his feet. So let us have no more of this questing for our presuppositions. Let us simply ask (and honestly answer) what it is we are assuming in whatever it is we do.

I happen to agree with Raschke that *questing* for presuppositions is pagan. The pagan wants to go off to search for God, when our God is actually near to us, in our hearts and in our mouths. The pagan quest is actually an attempt to get away from the omnipresent triune God of the Bible. His image in us is not entirely defaced by sin, and that standing reminder of His holiness is too much for us. And so the pagan quest begins—not to find presuppositions, but rather to find *different* presuppositions, presuppositions more to our sinful liking.

The problem with paganism is not that it is in this desperate hunt for certainty, but rather that it wants a different kind of certainty, an idolatrous certainty. In order to achieve this, rebellious man must escape from the God-given creational certainty that afflicts him in every thoughtful moment.

"Because that which may be known of God is *manifest in them*; for God hath shewed it unto them. For the invisible things of him from the creation of the world are clearly seen, *being understood* by the things that are made, even his eternal power and Godhead; so that they are *without excuse*" (Rom. 1:19-20). The problem of sinful man is not that he wants certainty. He already has it and he *doesn't like it*. The problem is that he wants his own certainty, or, failing that, his own uncertainty. But at whatever cost, short of repentance, it must be his *own*.

But on Raschke's stated principles, what is wrong with such outright paganism? Is this rejection of outright paganism an infallible presupposition of Raschke's? Is his rejection of foundationalism at a presuppositional level? If not, what is? Are his presuppositions, whatever they are, fallible? Infallible? If he is saying that to *pursue* presuppositions is idolatrous, then I agree. But if he is saying that merely to *have* them is the problem, then he is spiraling downward into incoherence, because he is urging upon us the presupposition that we are to have no presuppositions, the proposition that there aren't any.

CHAPTER 5

Knowledge and Blood

We have to avoid all forms of unbelief, whether in modernist or postmodernist guise. This requires a distinctive Trinitarian epistemology. Consider this some preliminary doodling on the subject.

One of the problems with this kind of discussion is that it tends to be limited to academics, and epistemic certainty becomes something you can demonstrate (or not) in a classroom. Reduced to this, certainty becomes a function of personality, logical acumen, bombast, and so on. But what about epistemology in the Bible? While it is lawful to discuss such things in a classroom, and (with direct permission from the Holy Spirit) it might be okay to write a book on it, things look very different in Scripture.

In the Bible, when the Word comes, the faithful are described as *receiving* it, or as *believing* it, or as *bearing witness* to it. It is a matter of *testimony* (John 3:33; 1 John 5:10). And certainty is measured in these life terms, it is measured in blood, and most emphatically not measured in terms of haunting self-doubts. When we begin with the problems of interpretation, we often never get to what the Bible presents so breezily, which is faith. When we begin with faith, we come to understanding. The fear of the Lord is the beginning of knowledge, not the goal of it.

How certain am I that in the observance of the Lord's Supper, the bread and wine do not turn into the literal flesh and blood of Jesus? In a classroom discussion, how can I answer this question? I could hold my hands apart six inches and say, "This much," or perhaps, in a rhetorical flourish, I could stretch my arms all the way out and say, "*This* much." But the martyrs who suffered under Bloody Mary had a different calculus entirely (and a far more biblical one). They sealed their testimony *with their blood*.

Related to this (the flip side of it, really) concerns what you are willing to kill for. A number of years ago, I served on a jury in a murder trial. We convicted the accused man, and the biblical standard we were operating with was that we had to be convinced "beyond a reasonable doubt." But note how loaded with epistemological concerns that phrase is. Beyond a reasonable doubt—what is *that*? But since this was a jury room, and not a classroom, we were dealing, in principle, with a man's life. How certain must we be *then*? The same principles are involved in going to war, drafting certain kinds of legislation, and so on.

We are called to believe, receive, bear witness, and *act*. When we act, there will be costs (at least in the real world). The issues of certainty are always issues that always revolve around cost. The problem with modernism is that it was willing to act on false principles and a false foundation, not bearing witness to Christ, and therefore it has been convicted of epistemic arrogance. But the problem with postmodernism is an *identical* one—it is also not willing to believe the story of Christ's *actual* resurrection from the dead, a story that therefore defines and subordinates all other stories. To use their jargon, if Christ's resurrection is not a metanarrative, a *reigning* metanarrative, then we are all still in our sins. And since the postmodern "incredulity to all metanarratives" includes this, it is also convicted of the arrogance of unbelief.

Some assume that if I attack postmodern epistemology, I must be doing so as a foundationalist. But I don't remember ever saying anything like that, and do remember saying quite a bit to the contrary. I don't think that we can take a series of indubitable legos and stack them up into a worldview. What we need around here is a Trinitarian epistemology, one that is not beholden to the arrogance of Descartes, and that is *equally* not beholden to the arrogance of the postmodernists. And just in passing, at bottom, it is *always the same arrogance.* Postmodernism is just modernism's ugly little brother in drag. Modernism says that God cannot have spoken, "because I have spoken to the contrary." Postmodernism says that God cannot have spoken, because "nobody *speaks* really, when you think about it." The key thing they share (and which the Bible calls unbelief) is wrapped up in that phrase "God cannot have spoken."

Do I resent postmodernism because it "imposes limitations on [my] dramatic epistemic self-confidence"? What is to prevent us from saying that a true epistemic humility leads a godly person not to question

Jesus and the Bible, but rather to question one's own finite and sinful interpretations?

Well, this. We should want a sure word from God. I want firm traction in a slippery place. I want light in the darkness. Let the one who speaks, the apostle Peter says, speak as the very oracle of God. We are living in perilous times, and we cannot afford to be without God's clear direction for us—clear direction for us in worship, in bringing up our children faithfully, in holding to what the Bible says about qualifications in pastors and elders, in transforming culture all the way down to the ground, and learning the difference between good rock and roll and bad rock and roll. No neutrality, and take no prisoners. I don't believe it is epistemic arrogance to listen when God speaks.

A man who leads with his own finite and sinful interpretations will find out soon enough that this is a universal corrosive, and now he does not know whether he is finite or sinful. He will soon find it impossible *not* to question Jesus and the Bible.

The problem is *not* that some Christians are now telling us that the Bible is more than a bundle of propositions. We know that, and have been saying it for years. I myself have been pummeling the epistemology of the Enlightenment (with shouts of exuberant joy) for some time now. But then along come some evangelical *poseurs*, using the obvious faults of modernism as a pretext for adopting something just as bad and twice as silly. So I says to myself, I says, let us rise up and smite that new thing, hip and thigh. Let us hew it to pieces before the Lord.

The Bible presents a grand story, a narrative. But here is the rub. We believe the story, we receive it. We bear witness to it. It is *the* story. It is the ultimately *true* story.

This is a Trinitarian epistemology because Jesus is the full revelation of God, the exact image of His being. God revealed Himself in Christ. If you have seen Me, Jesus said to Phillip, you have seen the Father. And Jesus, among many other things, was the First Witness, the Faithful Witness, the Preeminent Martyr. How certain was He of His identity? How firm was His grasp of those tricky passages in Isaiah about the suffering servant? And when the voice came from heaven, and others heard only thunder, how can we measure His response? In short, how do we evaluate Christ's epistemology? His blood not only saved His people, but His blood also showed us a way of knowing. We are to imitate Him.

CHAPTER 6

The Devil's Dictionary

When we consider the question of how we can know the truth, know what is lovely, and know what is good, we frequently neglect to address the more fundamental issue, which is the nature of the knowers. We assume certain things about the problem of knowledge, and this drives the solutions we come up with. We think the problem is a problem of *knowing*, when it is actually a problem of *knowers*.

This is just another way of saying that the study of epistemology is the result of sin. The seraphim that cry *holy, holy, holy* around the throne room of God do not have any problem grasping who they are and what they are doing there. The entrance of sin has brought about the antithesis (between the promised seed of the serpent and seed of the woman), and these two seeds know according to their respective natures. Because their respective natures are different, they challenge one another, and the challenge each presents to the other is in the realm of knowing.

"Did God really say that?" the serpent wanted to know. "How do you *know*?" From the very beginning, it has been the devil's question, and he loves to ask it of us. But when the devil asks me the meaning of a word, I don't mind answering the question. I do mind looking it up in his dictionary.

St. John is the patron saint of epistemology. That is, he is patron saint of a biblical approach to *believing* and *knowing*. He is not the patron saint of unbelieving epistemology. How do we know? How do we know that we know? These are reasonable questions to ask at the foot of the cross—and nowhere else.

We believe so that we may know. We must believe the truth, however, and not believe a lie. We are utterly dependent upon the grace of God in this. We cannot save ourselves; we cannot protect ourselves; we cannot know ourselves. Unless we know God, we cannot understand ourselves or our knowing. And if we come to know God, it is by means of His sheer gift, and then we have the mind of Christ. When this happens, all things come into focus.

The serpent, subtle as ever, wants to push back behind this faith, and wants us to inquire into the "philosophical preconditions" for believing. He needs to put his epistemology of unbelief *somewhere*. The epistemology of unbelief says that it wants to understand in order that it might believe. This is theologically incoherent, but more importantly, it is a lie. What it actually means is that a man "wants to understand, so he can gum up the argumentation of understanding, so that he doesn't have to believe." To this, St. John calls us to believe in Jesus, the Light that has come into the world. And in this believing, we will come to know.

When this is stated, all the philosophy departments set up the baying of their hounds, "Fideism!"—which is quite a mouthful for a hound. But those who believe know that fideism is just another form of unbelief. And how do they know? They have believed in Jesus Christ.

Fundamental assumptions are like the backs of our heads. We all have one, and none of us can see our own. One of the most exasperating features of working through literature on postmodernism is the fact that, for all the talk, the postmodernists couldn't deconstruct their way out of a paper bag.

One basic assumption underlying all forms of humanism, whether it is an optimistic humanism or not, is the assumption that epistemology is a generic problem for "humans." We all have to answer the same questions, the thinking goes, and we all have to submit to the same puzzles. But the Bible does not teach this—rather, it teaches that from the very beginning, God has divided the rebellious race of men into two categories, and these two groups *know differently*. God promised constant enmity between the seed of the woman and the seed of the serpent. The Scriptures tell us that these two seeds have a different "language," a different "hermeneutic," a different epistemology.

The seed of the woman have an epistemology of obedience that makes no sense to the unbeliever. Jesus put it this way: "If any man will do his will, he shall know of the doctrine, whether it be of God, or whether I speak of myself" (John 7:17). What is the Lord saying here? He is telling us that the one who is willing to obey will *know*. The one who is not willing to obey will *not* know. So then, Bob's your uncle. The Bible most emphatically does *not* promise a single way of knowing to all men. The assumption that there must be this common humanistic bond is actually an assumption that rules out the Christian faith from the outset.

This is why there is *always* room to doubt—for doubters. The unbeliever does not find the evidence compelling. He sees cracks and crevices in the argument. But he does so because he does not wish to repent. For example, Richard Rorty knew that only "a theism that combined a God with equal measures of truth, love, and justice, could do the trick. But since I could not imagine myself being religious, and had indeed become more raucously secular, I did not consider that to be an option for me." Note that phrase—*could not imagine.* As with so many other things, it again comes down to this—a failure of imagination.

This is why believers find many things compelling (as they ought) that leave unbelievers with philosophical problems spun tight around their axle. The word *semiotics* comes from the Greek word for signs, which were the miracles that Jesus did in front of people. And when He did them in front of people, some were convinced by the semiotic display, and some were not convinced. Those who were not convinced were prevented from coming to faith by their *sin.*

The first witnesses of the resurrection of Jesus Christ (the guards) had an amazing bit of information on their hands. But what did they do with the sign? They ran off and took a bribe to suppress the truth of what had happened. Had they been willing to obey, they would have known that Christ was from God. But as it was, a man came back from the dead, *on their watch*, and they still couldn't figure it out.

Another humanistic assumption in epistemological discussion is the assumption that human language is somehow a human construct. In his discussion of the limits of human discourse about God, Carl Raschke talks as though human discourse about God is a function of theological speculation only. But human language is not just a carrier of the latest postmodern hooey from the academy, it is also the carrier of Isaiah's prophetic utterance, through which God Himself is speaking in human language.

To argue that human language is inherently limited *sounds* humble, but it is really impudence on stilts. Suppose a man is chained to a dungeon wall, and he demonstrates to his cell mate, beyond all reasonable doubt, that they cannot touch the jailer's nose. It does not follow from this, I would like to maintain, that the jailer cannot touch *their* noses. Perhaps human language was a creation and gift of God. Perhaps God *designed* it to talk about Him and to commune with Him. Maybe it isn't a rickety jumble of linguistic sticks. From the ancient humanist (and sophistical) boast that man is the measure of all things, we have now come to the end of the postmodern *cul de sac*. "Man is the muddle of all things."

But not if he is willing to obey Jesus.

CHAPTER 7

Bright Red Orthodoxy

The postmodernists have climbed into the car of modernity's premises, and have driven it into a tree. What the postmodernists do not appear to grasp, however, is that mumbling incoherently to oneself in the wreckage of that old car does not constitute having a new car. Not even if you say *vrooom* to yourself and imagine that you are toodling down the road, bottle of Jack Daniels still intact and still in hand.

But then along come some evangelical Christians who (for *some* inscrutable reason, best known to themselves) want to identify themselves with the postmodernists. What they are doing is slowing down their vintage Mercedes of Trinitarian Bright Red Orthodoxy, with not a scratch on it, to do a little rubber-necking at the accident. "With a little epistemic humility, there is quite a bit we could probably learn from that learned fellow! And if we crawled in there with him, we could crawl back out again. And then we would be an Emergent Church, emerging (but not too far!) from the Shattered Windshield of Modernity!"

Christians should not overstate our opportunities in this. Postmodernism is only a good development in the same way that the prodigal son envying the pig food was a good development. The point is for him to return to the Father, and not to acquire a taste for the food in the trough.

One of the most frustrating aspects of reading modern evangelical writers, especially those who are attempting some sort of relevant edgy thing, is the inability of such writers to see themselves in a broad historical context. They have no x on a map of church history that says, "You are here." Nothing is more irrelevant than such relevance, nothing duller than evangelical edginess, and nothing more *predictable* than an evangelical writer trying to get us all to long for "something more." Nothing is more historically opaque than this apparent evangelical transparency. The "something more" comes in many different packages, but in the evangelical world *it always comes.*

The modern evangelical schtick is to be dissatisfied with traditional forms, and the traditional form of modern evangelicalism is to figure out how to walk away from the last traditional form, even if the *last* traditional form was created by evangelicals walking away from the form before that. All postmodernism has done for historically-orphaned evangelicals is make us change the timing of our cycles. Winds of doctrine change direction more quickly than they used to. Our turnaround times are quicker now. The fads that speed through the evangelical world now are like that "on-demand" low inventory system that Walmart has. What used to take forty years to spend itself now takes around five.

And nobody appears to know that in pursuing the "new thing" they are doing nothing more or less than perpetuating the "old thing." And this particular tradition of ours is genuinely destructive.

A new kind of Christian. What kind of tradition is necessary to make it possible for such a phrase to even begin to be attractive? And why is it that modern evangelicals cannot see that walking away from tradition *is their tradition*? If this were a postmillennial longing for the maturing of the new man, a longing for maturity itself, then the story would be different. But it isn't, and evangelicalism continues to wander, clueless. Someone is going to write a history of modern evangelicalism someday. They should call it *Gullible's Travels*.

Modernity's wrecked car was the car of abstractions, and it could run, but their problem was that they didn't believe in a factory that could manufacture any such thing.

Abstractions don't exist, if by existence you mean having a certain weight or color. Neither do propositions, if by existence you mean material embodiment. And of course, by such criteria, God the Father doesn't exist either.

But of course, abstractions still *function* just fine, provided the people using them are grounded in an incarnational and Trinitarian life of faith and obedience. And when people are not living that way, abstractions are death, not only of the abstracting one, but also of many millions of others (caught in the maw of modernity). Liberty, equality, and fraternity, as non-existent abstractions, have still slain their tens of thousands. Of course, on the other hand, abstractions have done a lot of good. Love, for example, is kind, and gentle. But not to anyone in particular; to be kind to someone in particular would have gotten love, the abstract noun, chucked out of 1 Corinthians 13.

So abstractions are necessary to good, healthy, concrete life in the world as God gave it to us. "Mowing the lawn is best when followed by a cold beer" is an abstraction just like "beauty without truth is as limp as truth without beauty is ugly."

"Abstractions are bad" is a sentence which entirely depends for its sense on a robust and very healthy abstraction. So obviously, when we lament the bad effects of abstractions in philosophy and theology (and there are many such bad effects), we are actually talking about abstractions when used in a certain way, or abstractions that are given ontological zip code status up in Platoville. But abstractions when used rightly, on the other hand, are a blessing of the first rank. An honest answer is like a kiss on the lips, says Proverbs, but since this is an abstraction, nothing actually lands on the lips. And it is not even a shame.

Because they are not willing to traffic honestly with propositions and abstractions, we should not be surprised to find emergent thinkers saying that they advocate a move from the "absolute to the authentic." But of course, the fact that these are a couple of adjectives being used as abstractions means that we do not yet know what we are talking about. Moving from the "absolute" to the "authentic" blends right in with the current *kulturesmog* since no one appears to feel the urge to ask what this is supposed to mean. Absolute *what* to authentic *what*? Absolute fraud to authentic integrity?

How about absolute triune personality to authentic peach pits?

This sort of undefined thing is a marketing ploy, and works the way all marketing ploys do. What sounds good to the shopper, and, because he is in the grip of feeling good, will cause him to neglect the asking of pertinent questions. In the fifties bread was marketed with labels like *enriched*, which meant that they put the same kind of stuff in your bread that they put into linoleum somewhere during the manufacturing process. Today we market bread with very different phrases like *all natural*, which means that they put the same kind of stuff in your bread without running it through the filters first. Because, after all, if you go back far enough, linoleum is an "all natural" product.

After all, the ingredients are not summoned up *ex nihilo*. Everything came from somewhere, and that somewhere was natural at some point. But nobody asks questions because *all natural* makes us feel at one with the rhythms of the earth. For the same reason we like to buy food that is "chemical free." Really? What is it made of then? Any day now I expect someone to successfully market some organic food that is "free of all molecules." Anyway, I know I am digressing, but there is a point here. People buy into slogans when they ought to *think* for a minute.

Absolute to authentic. Huh. Why not inauthentic to authentic? That would at least imply that whatever noun this is modifying should be the same noun. Inauthentic Thai food to authentic Thai food might be a worthwhile move. But "absolute to authentic" is just a hand-waving sham. If you don't like absolutes in ethics, aesthetics, or theology, then go ahead and say so—but only if you are willing to refrain from the use of any absolutes in the condemnation. In other words, it is not possible to damn absolutes because damning is way too . . . absolute. The relativist, having nowhere to stand, can only summon up enough power to hecky-darn the absolutes. Fortunately, the absolutes pay no attention whatever.

From inauthentic art collections to authentic art collections makes sense. And absolute certainty to uncertainty makes sense too. I can go with that. But absolute to authentic? This just plain baffles me. It is like asking whether ice cream has no bones and the higher they fly the much.

Although it makes no sense, it still communicates something—just like the "all natural" communicates something. But what it communicates is a blurry feeling, and not anything that means anything with clarity or precision. And what this move is trying to get us to *feel*, in that blurry, sentimental postmodern way, is that dogmatic people are inveterate frauds. For did we not move from absolute (people) to authentic (people)? Okay, deal me in. I'll play this game. I would like to propose a new absolute: *authentic people are good people.* This is my proposed absolute. Any takers? Is this right, or not? If it is, then we haven't actually moved from absolute to authentic, for to embrace authenticity is to embrace this new absolute. But if it is not right, then why do we want to leave our absolutes if we are not going to become good people by so doing? Hey?

But I was not proposing my absolute as a mere *reductio.* I really believe that this is a true absolute, grounded in the absolute law of God, which in its turn is grounded in the nature of the divine being. We are to be perfect as our heavenly Father is perfect. We are to be authentic, for in Him is no shadow or variation due to change. This is true at all times, in all cultures, every day of the week, 24-7, and to be promulgated in every single Sunday School class, world without end. In short, it is true. It is an absolute.

Consequently, I want to chase this movement back into the hole it is emerging from because in their hostility to absolutes, they are a profound enemy of every virtue they say they are advancing. Are we to be humble? Not absolutely. Authentic? More or less, for now. Relational? Until the next big advance in theology and cultural surrender.

Those who have embraced the emergent jargon can therefore be grouped into two categories—the first would be those who have been taken in by *false alternatives*. Absolute or authentic? Do you want to buy five yards of cloth or *blue* cloth? Dark beer or beer *in a glass*? The second category would be those who are liars and scoundrels, as inauthentic as it gets.

Do I therefore oppose authenticity? Absolutely not.

CHAPTER 8

Against Philosophy

I n the course of pursuing this little postmodern jag of mine, reading folks I wouldn't ordinarily read, I have been struck with how much postmodernists share in common with the modernity they *think* they are rejecting. Shared assumptions leap off the page, invisible both to them and their modernist targets. Here are some obvious shared assumptions:

Language is a human creation.

Everyone simply assumes that our ability to speak is something that separates us from God, rather than a gift that God gave us so that we might commune with Him. But where does this assumption come from? It comes from the sinful heart of man who wants to *attain* to God on his own (or not, as the case may be). Self-righteousness, and particularly the priggish intellectual self-righteousness that wants to figure it all out autonomously, cannot acknowledge that God gave us all that we need to love and adore Him, and that included the gift of speaking. The thing that separates us from God is our sinful distaste of the holy, and *not* our creaturely limitations. The problem is sin, not linguistic boundaries.

Humanity is one.

But Scripture teaches that there is a difference between how the sheep know and how the goats "know." In a fallen world, there is no epistemology that will be satisfactory to all, or equally compelling to all. The fundamental divide between faith and unbelief is a basic epistemological divide. The sheep hear and believe because they are His sheep. The goats cannot believe because they are not His sheep. This means that the eschatological doctrines of Heaven and Hell are basic to all biblical epistemology.

If the orthodox Christian faith is true, then there are two types of knowing, one of them autonomous and spurious. To assume a unified epistemology is therefore at bottom to assume that the Christian faith is false. Christians who assume this without reflection are then placed in the unenviable position of trying to persuade other people that the faith is true, building their case on the bedrock assumption that this same faith is false. And this is how the endeavor of apologetics so easily comes a cropper.

Philosophy is trustworthy.

However much the postmodernists quibble about modernist schools of thought, and however much they might want to pretend that Derrida is a writer, not a philosopher, they are all doing the same basic thing. Philosophy is nothing more than "smart guys speculating about the world and screwing it all up." And by *that* definition, the postmodernists are just another verse of the same, tired song.

Jesus tells some of His questioners that they should believe on the basis of His works. In other words, Jesus said that ordinary people should look at one of His signs (say, water to wine) and they should draw the conclusion from that work or sign that He was indeed the Light of God that has come into the world, in order to shine on every man. Jesus said that He presented evidence conclusive enough to damn those who rejected it. Now, imagine any of our current word-manglers there on the spot.

Modernists: "How does the doctrine that Jesus is the Son of God follow logically from the datum that water turned into wine? Formulate that in an argument, please."

Postmodernists: "The narrative of water to wine is compelling indeed, but we cannot allow it to be privileged above other narratives. To do so would return us to the hegemony of Enlightenment categories, and would take a particular incident in Cana, and would totalize on *that* basis for the rest of the world. Which is, again, Enlightenment hubris."

Steward of the feast who had believed things about the entire universe on such scanty evidence: "What's the Enlightenment? All I know is that was the best wine I ever had, and Jesus did it. He must be the Son of God!"

The gospel is spread through authoritative and dogmatic proclamation, and does not have to have its papers stamped by the philosophers before it is allowed to proceed. We Christians have not taken seriously enough the warnings of the New Testament against vain philosophy and the cunning deceitfulness of men (and serpents). In his famous warnings in 1 Corinthians and Colossians, Paul was not warning us about Stoicism or Epicureanism in *particular*, but rather about a worldly turn of mind, of which those two philosophies were just two samples. That worldly turn of mind is still with us, still wrecking havoc in the Church, still seducing simpletons, and still making smart people think that polysyllabic jargon constitutes wisdom. But with all their knowing, they did not know God (1 Cor. 1:21). Philosophy as such is a pursuit for goats, and this is another reason it frequently ends up in lechery.

This does not mean that Christians cannot be philosophically informed; some Christians should be. But all Christians who are philosophically informed and literate have a moral duty to hate what they are studying. I am glad that our society has poison control centers, and that there are people who study various toxins and poisons. But if they ever come to love their toxins, then it is time to start worrying.

Here is one example of the kind of exasperating false dilemma and blurry thinking that smart guys consistently perpetrate. I ran into this one in Raschke's book on why evangelicals must embrace postmodernity. One of his points was that we must abandon propositional fixity in order to focus on *relationship*. But of course, one of our central duties in healthy relationships is to *talk sense* in them. What would a man's relationship with his wife be like without intelligible propositions? "We have $553.25 in the bank. And two bills over that amount due tomorrow." I can assure you that the health of the relationship is dependent upon a coherent world, the kind of world created by the triune God—in other words, the kind of world we live in.

People in relationship don't radiate "relationally" at one another across the room. They *talk*. If we were

to take all their conversation, "debone" it of all propositions, we would have ourselves one raggedy mess of a
relationship lying on the floor.

CHAPTER 9

How the Cow Ate the Cabbage

Trying to bring a little moisture into our dogmas concerning Scripture, Carl Raschke's words drip like cold water from the roof of a damp cave. Taking Charles Hodge to task for his stalwart defense of the doctrine of Scripture, Raschke says this:

> Hodge essentially made the unprecedented claim that the saga of the parting of the Red Sea, Elijah's miracle on Mount Carmel, or Jesus' ascension all had the same ontological status as the rain in Spain or the annual flowering of the cherry blossoms in the nation's capital. In other words, God's extraordinary acts in history were really quite ordinary. There was no room for the Reformer's faith response to Scripture. Faith was really rather incidental.*

The intellectual dishonesty involved in this really takes the breath away. Rascke is arguing that Hodge is making no room for faith when it comes to these events. And *why*? Because Hodge *believes* that they happened. And he, Raschke, leaving room for an ontological status other than that of "having happened" is really exhibiting

---

* Carl Raschke, *The Next Revolution: Why Evangelicals Must Embrace Post-modernity* (Grand Rapids: Baker Academic, 2004), 123–4.

faith because he doesn't think it necessary to believe they really happened. The death of faith is apparently to be found in believing things.

So. God says something like Jesus was "parted from them, and carried up into heaven" (Luke 24:51). Are you ready for the deep mysteries of the postmodern way? Ready for the deep things of Satan? If someone reads this and thinks that this is what *actually* happened, it only shows that he is in the grip of Aristotle, Descartes, and other unsavory characters. However, if someone else doesn't believe it, this shows that he understands the immense depths that the adventure of faith may take us down to . . . and all without an air hose. Faith is now unbelief and unbelief is now faith. Jeepers. One more postmodern idea grinder up against the word of the Lord.

Then there is his use of the word "unprecedented." Hodge made the *unprecedented* move of thinking that the historical events described in the Bible really happened? This was a nineteenth century development? Luke went to Princeton (Luke 1:1-4)?

Raschke's view of an extraordinary event is one that did not necessarily happen. "Honey, an extraordinary thing happened to me today. I was kidnapped by aliens over the lunch hour, and made to listen to old Neil Diamond albums." "Really?" "No, not *really*. But *that's* what makes this story so unique. One might even say extraordinary. And this is what makes this story so important to me personally."

I'll tell you what is extraordinary—so much so that I am almost tempted to give up my belief that the age of miracles is past. What is extraordinary is that our ecclesiastical solons are giving these people the time of day. These guys are getting their books *published*.

Evangelical postmodernists luxuriate in the sensation that they are on the bleeding, cutting edge. They feel that they have the "out-there-ness" to really make a radical statement to our times. In reality, their story is about as interesting as the one about how the cow ate the cabbage. By now, I have read a goodish bit of their stuff, and the excited breathlessness over a bunch of nothing reminds me of a story. It is not exactly a metanarrative, but it serves a purpose.

I have two uncles who have an impish streak, one of them a minister and the other a psychologist. One time they decided to do something that would illustrate the power of jargon, and the experiment succeeded *nobly*. They took a bunch of vocabulary from a journal of psychology, cut it all up into individual words, and put different kinds of words in four different cans. The nouns went in one can, the verbs in another, the adverbs in another, and the adjectives in the fourth. They then sat down to "write an article." Typing "The," they then reached into the appropriate can, pulled out the kind of word they needed and typed it in. One of my uncles said that the scary thing was that the article they wrote this way hovered perpetually on the threshold of sense. When my other uncle gave it to a colleague, asking him to review it for him, the response he got was, "Harold, that's *deep*."

I understand that there are web sites now that will perform this kind of jargon-generation much more rapidly, in case you are up for tenure and having some trouble getting published.

In dealing with all this *deep* postmodern stuff, it is hard to escape the notion that a goodly number of people involved have been educated beyond their intelligence. They don't see that heaps and piles of jargon reveal nothing more than heaps and piles of jargon. And those who are not in over their heads are sinister. Try this one on from Raschke's book. "Just as Einstein's construct of 'curved space' within a space-time 'continuum' resisted common sense, yet worked well mathematically, so Deleuze's suggestion of 'curved concepts' within a plane of immanence may function more felicitously than any paradigm of predication."

Exactly. I myself have had it up to *here* with infelicitous paradigms of predication not stepping aside to curved concepts when they want their turn on the plane of immanence. Also, I don't like how ice cream cartons tear off when you try to open them, leaving little strips of paper lying on the ice cream. You know?

CHAPTER 10

Dumpster Diving in Egypt

Whenever believers confront unbelieving cultures, the perennial question arises—what can and cannot be taken from them and used by us in the advancement of the kingdom? One of the most enduring illustrations of what to do here is the image given by one of the early church fathers, which is that of plundering the Egyptians. When Israel came out of Egypt, they did so with many Egyptian treasures, treasures that were subsequently used in the building of the tabernacle. And this is a great image—we ought to use it more, and apply additional aspects of the metaphor. I say this because of the temptation that many contemporary Christians have to plunder gold from the postmodernists. And this is fine, provided we remember two important points related to the process.

When do you plunder the enemy? Well, you do so *after* you have defeated him. You do not get to do this simply because you are "against" your enemy. You have to actually defeat him. When did the Israelites take this gold from the Egyptians? This occurred after the superpower of Egypt was a smoking helicopter on the ground, blades sticking out at grotesque angles. The Lord Jesus followed this reasonable procedure as well—He did not take the strong man's goods until after He had bound him securely. *Then* He plundered the house.

But there are a good many confused souls who, in the name of plundering the enemy, are actually fraternizing with the enemy. I have no problem taking insights from the postmodernists. But I don't think we ought to do it until after the cathedral is built, and Derrida's visage can be found on one or more of our gargoyles.

This is related to the second point, which is, *what do we plunder?* If we are confused about our need to be loyal to Christ above all, in all, and through all, we will have a tendency to take "gold" from the Egyptians that is not gold at all. In the name of plundering the Egyptians, we will actually be dumpster diving in Egypt. Sure, take *gold* from the Egyptians. But at this point in time, those who are urging the church to avail ourselves of all this gold are not setting the kind of example that inspires me to confidence. "Let us take gold from the Egyptians!" say they, and yet when I look in the rusty shopping cart they are pushing away from Memphis, all I can see is Holiday Inn towels with holes in them, used grapefruit rinds, some Elvis knick-knacks, and some old Tarantino videos.

CHAPTER 11
One Foot Nailed to the Floor

Chesterton once said (Chesterton *always* once said) that the purpose of an open mind was the same as the purpose of an open mouth—it is meant to *close* on something. A man who is not closed in certain respects is a man who was never open in the right kind of way. The apostle Paul once took a jab at a certain kind of woman who did not know this glorious truth, the kind who was always learning and never coming to a knowledge of the truth. Always learning and never arriving.

This principle is important because those of us who are involved in the resurgence of classical and Christian education are not doing this in a void. We are seeking to reestablish this particular kind of education in a postmodern world, one that has lost all its fundamental moorings, which means, I guess, come to think of it, that we *are* trying to do this in a void.

So we really have to watch our step. A perennial temptation for bookish types has always been to enjoy the peace and quiet of the ivory tower. This temptation is ancient, but the world of postmodern flux has given studious types even greater incentives to avoid landing in the truth. Coming to the truth has always been like coming to a lit stick of dynamite. And it has always been the case that quiet academicians (like Calvin) have felt pressure to study the truth in such a way as to avoid colliding with the reigning orthodoxy. And that was Calvin's intention until Farel's hair-curling exhortation that prevailed upon him to remain in Geneva. Searching for the truth faithfully might get you unaligned with the prevailing lie, and so there have always been reasons for keeping your head low. One good way to keep your head low has always been to shove your nose in a book.

But today, we do not so much have a prevailing orthodoxy as a pandemonium of prevailing orthodoxies, and the one epistemological rule is that you must not speak any kind of final word. The pandemonium, the pluralism, the polytheism, must be preserved. You *may* have (indeed, you must have) a place at the table with all the other chattering professors at the University of Athens, but you must never declare that Jesus is Lord over the whole business.

Now throw the resurgence of classical Christian education into this postmodern whirl. There are two ways to approach the situation. One is the way of faithfulness. This is to maintain the antithesis, where the Mars Hill encounter is not to simply add the voice of Paul to that of the Epicureans and Stoics, but rather to *declare* the ultimate and final alternative. What Paul says in this hubbub of polytheism called Athens is striking: ". . . but now commandeth all men every where to repent: because he hath appointed a day, in the which he will judge the world in righteousness by that man whom he hath ordained; whereof he hath given assurance unto all men, in that he hath raised him from the dead" (Acts 17:30b-31). Note the words: commands, repent, appointed, judge, righteousness, ordained, *assurance*. Because, Paul did *not* add, "this is what works for me."

The other alternative is to treat classical Christian education as one option among many, kind of like the resurgence of retro swing dancing a few years back. In the tornado of postmodern relativism, *lots* of things fly by. There is a cow, for example, and then there is a Honda Accord, and *there* goes a classical Christian school. Here in the tornado, we have lots of options, and ain't it grand? The central characteristic of this kind of classical approach is to go through life with your mouth open, but never to close on anything, never to say, "Ah, at last! *This* is the truth." The point is endless discussion, to be always learning and never coming to a knowledge of the Truth Himself.

The liberal cleric in hell in C.S. Lewis' *The Great Divorce* thinks this way, and Lewis nails it for what it is—empty posturing.

"... for I will bring you to the land not of questions but of answers, and you shall see the face of God."

"Ah, but we must all interpret those beautiful words in our own way! For me there is no such thing as a final answer. The free wind of inquiry must *always* continue to blow through the mind, must it not? 'Prove all things' ... to travel hopefully is better than to arrive."

"If that were true, and known to be true, how could anyone travel hopefully? There would be nothing to hope for."

"But you must feel yourself that there is something stifling about the idea of finality? Stagnation, my dear boy, what is more soul-destroying than stagnation?"

"You think that, because hitherto you have experienced truth only with the abstract intellect. I will bring you where you can taste it like honey and be embraced by it as by a bridegroom. Your thirst shall be quenched."

"Well, really, you know, I am not aware of a thirst for some ready-made truth which puts an end to intellectual activity in the way you seem to be describing. Will it leave me the free play of Mind, Dick? I must insist on that, you know."

"Free, as a man is free to drink while he is drinking. He is not free still to be dry." The Ghost seemed to think for a moment. "I can make nothing of that idea," it said.

And neither can our contemporaries make anything of that idea. But it is our task to experience it, know it, pursue it, love it, and teach it. And we have to teach it as though we wake up in the morning *knowing* that we believe it. The tepid tentativeness of emergent compromisers with postmodernity (whether that tentativeness is real or feigned does not really matter) is a profound capitulation. The same kind of tentativeness is found in those classical Christian educators who want to discuss everything endlessly, one foot nailed to the floor. In short, there are classical Christian educators who are comfortable in our current setting precisely because they are as postmodern as anybody else around here.

In a relativistic world, anything goes—except any serious challenge of that relativistic world. For yourself, you can do anything you want, and it is encouraged and applauded, no matter how weird. But there is a difference between teaching Latin because "Jesus is Lord" and teaching Latin because "it takes all kinds."

Good schools are full of truth claims. Godly schools are full of truth claims. Classical Christian schools are full of truth claims. But to pretend that there are severe philosophical problems with all "truth claims," and to avoid declaring the truth (as in, unapologetically) because of feigned problems with "arid propositionalism" is to simply provide an excuse to those who want to turn their head away from the offered *honey*.

It is not possible to love Jesus Christ without loving the propositions about Him revealed to us by God. We are to love the *words* of God, and if we do not, we do not love the Word of God. We all know of the punctilious scribe, who substitutes true words for the Word, but it is no improvement to go the emergent route, and substitute confused words for the Word. We are to come to God through Christ, and this means *using the means provided to us*. One of the means (not the only means, but one of them) would be the great blessing of dogmatic truth claims. "Jesus died for my sins. Jesus walked on the water. Jesus is the only way to the Father. Jesus cleansed the Temple." All these are what arcane investigators of paranormal phenomena call true statements. We can put them in the bank. We can teach them to our children, in every classroom. We can declare them to the world. We can stand in them, or sit on them. And, in these pressing times, we can refuse to apologize for their dogmatic and blunt character. We can give Rorty and Derrida the raspberry. We are Christians, and are not post-anything.

Is arid propositionalism a problem? Sure, and always has been. Are there "truth-oriented" classical Christian schools that do nothing but stuff dry facts into parched heads, with no experience of the sweetness of truth? Certainly, and that's bad. If you were to ask a certain man if you could meet his wife, and he pulled out a manila folder that was filled with data about her, and admitted that he had not actually talked with *her* for years, you would think you were in a conversation with a moral idiot. And the more propositional facts he substituted for direct knowledge of her, the worse you would think it.

But if a man had lived with his wife for years, and someone asked him one day what color her eyes were, he could not wave off the question with, "Oh, I think it is *much* more important to focus on I-Thou-relationship-encounters than on arid truth-claims. Analytic statements like 'her eyes are blue' or 'her eyes are green' are such *soulless* propositions, you know?" Yeah, right, you hoser.

"Even so faith, if it hath not propositions, is dead, being alone. Yea, a man may say, Thou hast faith, and I have propositions: shew me thy faith without thy propositions, and I will shew thee my faith by my propositions." Some might argue that this restatement is leaning in the opposite direction from James' expressed concerns. So it is, which does not make it false or unnecessary—Paul did that too. Paul and James were in full fellowship, both their concerns were legitimate, and they extended the right hand to one another. They did this, and what they both wrote is in the Scriptures because sinful men constantly want to veer off in one direction or the other. Paul opposed dead works, and James opposed dead faith. What they shared was their hostility to *death*.

In our recovery of classical and Christian education,

we are confronting all the same issues. We too are opposed to the death that unbelief always brings, however it is decked out. We are opposed to dead truth claims, and we are opposed to dead skepticism about truth claims. Modernity? Postmodernity? A plague on both your houses.

CHAPTER 12

Three Toddlers With Kazoos

M odern evangelicals have mastered the art of sugary compromise, and we like to call it balance, love, relevance, or something. With the establishment of a distinctive evangelical movement after the Second World War, the intent was to defend the central tenets of the Christian faith, but to do so in a way that was not pugnacious, like the fundamentalists were. Fundamentalism without the attitude—that was the ticket.

Evangelical leaders like Harold Ockenga, Carl Henry, and Billy Graham certainly looked like they had a winning formula. The flagship magazine *Christianity Today* was founded along with institutions like Fuller Seminary. Wheaton College, established in the previous century, was an evangelical bastion and an important part of this new spiritual weather-system. InterVarsity provided eager students from around the nation who filled the burgeoning ranks of an imposing movement. Although D. G. Hart has argued that evangelicalism as such does not really exist, it is difficult to assert that *nothing* was going on.

The evangelicals had a strong hand. But there is one thing that fundamentalists do well, better than anyone: they can follow an argument, and they can tell within fifteen minutes whether someone is gearing up to give away the store. So in dealing with the irrelevance of evangelical academia, the point here is to exclude from my discussion the ornery conservatives and fundamentalists. They have their own problems, including blinkered separatism and historical isolation, and among all the brethren of Christendom, they can be most exasperating. Their ranks were originally filled by the sons of the Scots and Scots-Irish, and the gifts of sweet reasonableness, as Coleridge once put it, have not been "vouchsafed to them at present." But the one problem they do *not* have is the perennial evangelical problem of lust for relevance and acceptance. They don't recoil from a fight. And because staunch conservatives don't care about relevance, in the long run they find themselves, well, far more relevant.

The evangelical problem goes back to the fatal desire to be "nice" fundamentalists, and this is why evangelicals have lost their center, their balance, their faith, and now their minds. Initially, the siren call of niceness had a good deal of appeal because the Scriptures do say that we are to be "speaking the truth *in love*," and that our speech should be "*gracious*, seasoned with salt."

But there was a disastrous mistake waiting for us here. Francis Schaeffer once used the telling image of a watershed. High in the Rocky Mountains you can find the continental divide and look at a spot of snow straddling that divide. And there, six inches apart (which is not far at all), you can see snow which will eventually find itself in the Gulf of Mexico, and just a few inches away, there is snow that will wind up in the Pacific Ocean. The six-inch spread *there* is far more significant than a six-inch spread just a few feet away.

So the problem was not that evangelicals wanted to hold to the central truths of the Christian faith in love. The problem was that love was defined in ways that did not line up with Scripture. Schaeffer also wrote memorably that "the mark of a Christian" is love. This *is* a non-negotiable center. We are supposed to speak the truth in love. In fact, if anyone disputes this—if any man does not love Jesus and does not love his neighbor—then may God damn him. This last expression, of course, gives us a case of the evangelical flutters, and we say that this way of speaking is *itself* a violation of the truth in the first part of the sentence. So perhaps we should say it this way: if any man does not love Jesus and does not love his neighbor, then may God damn him (1 Cor. 16:22).

The apostle Paul tells the Galatians not to bite and devour each other. They are to *love* one another. Those who would overthrow this love through self-important religiosity should go off and castrate themselves (Gal. 5:12). In short, Scripture makes it most plain—love is *not* what saccharine and sweety-nice evangelicals want to pretend it is. They say that love is everything, but then cannot explain it, define it, or live it. They say that to be scriptural, we must love, but then they revolt against the kind of love that Scripture models for us. So their problem is not that they want love; the problem is that they don't want it at all.

The desire of evangelicals to be relevant, engaged with culture, kind and gracious, approachable, and so on, is a desire (in the abstract) that can be applauded by all right-minded Christians. But this desire, even in the early stages, was six inches too far to the west. And this is why the evangelical establishment, particularly the evangelical establishment as now represented by its flagship colleges and publications, is completely adrift. Because they care about engaging with a culture that doesn't care about engaging with them back, the pressure is on to compromise over and over, again and again. Maybe this *next* sellout will get the world's attention.

Jesus said that desire for honor from men is a barrier to true faith in Him (Jn. 5:44). We are told to love not the world, or the things in the world—the lust of the flesh, the lust of the eyes, and the pride of life (1 Jn. 2:16-17). Is the pride of life a temptation to academics? To ask the question is to answer it. Friendship with the world is enmity with God (Jas. 4:4).

So what was the watershed issue? Love (which is most necessary) is to be defined *by God*, and not by unbelieving bedwetters and handwringers. When we decide whether or not we are being nice by whether or not the unbelieving establishment *says* we are being nice, the end result is that we will eventually find ourselves cheek by jowl with the unbelievers *in their unbelief*. For the sake of winning them, we allow ourselves to be won by them. Just like a simpleton teenage girl, we hope vainly to lure some horny boy into chastity, and the way we think it can be done is by lying down with him in the back seat of a car. What could go wrong?

That is the process, and so this is where the process has brought us. Evangelical colleges *routinely* accommodate themselves to theistic evolution, the ordination of women, pathetic views of Scripture, and postmodern hoohah, the last of which could be refuted by three toddlers with kazoos. These institutions do all this because they care what the world thinks of them; they do not trust in Christ the Lord because they care about all the wrong things. They give a rip, and the result is thundering irrelevance.

We in the American church have cycled downward into incoherent unbelief two times in the twentieth century. The first time was when the spirit of modernism captured the mainstream denominations, who allowed it in for the sake of relevance. And so, of course, those denominations promptly became irrelevant. Son of a gun. The second time is when the spirit of postmodernism captured the evangelical establishment, which happened some time ago, but like that simpleton girl we are now starting to show. This also was done for the sake of relevance. The times they are a changing, but of course, they didn't *really* change, and it turns out the devil still lies.

Biblical absolutism is therefore absolutely necessary, and without it, every evangelical college, university, and seminary is doomed to run through the same dreary downward spiral again. The problem with fundamentalism was not that it was absolutist, but rather that it was a form of truncated absolutism. What is necessary, at bottom, is a recovery of cosmic faith—faith in God, faith in Christ, faith in the Holy Spirit, faith in the Scriptures, faith in the Church, faith in the gospel, faith in history, faith in story, faith in the sacraments, faith in the inexorable and triumphant progress of the gospel throughout the world, with all of it rightly ordered in accordance with the Word. Any college without a robust and scrappy tenacity for such a statement of faith *as lived out in everything* is a college that is lost. By this measurement, many evangelical colleges today are adrift, but they are not really in a position to let their donors know about it.

Along with this necessary faith is a concomitant set of what we might call unbeliefs. What do we hold as inconsistent with what we affirm? What must an evangelical college defy? In what direction must true Christian higher education deliver the old raspberry? Lyotard defined postmodernism as "incredulity toward all metanarratives." Of course, this is a metanarrative itself, smirking away as though we wouldn't notice, and so all we need to do is summon the toddlers and their kazoos. But we can borrow one good thing from Lyotard (beyond his name): the belief that a central part of our recovery of sanity will be a recovery of incredulity. But incredulity toward what?

Christian higher education will not recover its soul or its sanity until it learns to greet any idea that originates in unbelief with a gut chuckle. And this means that we have to name names—and deal with those self-confessed evangelicals who specialize in decking out unbelief in sanctimonious terminology. A young man in our congregation recently told his father that sin was like a turd with powdered sugar on it, which exhibited wisdom far beyond the capacity of many evangelical academicians. In Christian higher education, toward what must we show our sanctified incredulity? We are evangelical educators, and so we do not believe in evolution, which is the view that Prince Charles used to be a frog. We do not believe that thinking the Bible in its entirety is infallible truth from God makes us indebted to the Enlightenment, for Pete's sake. We do not believe in bureaucracy, which is the barren soul of technocratic modernity. We do not believe in trendy evangelical feminism, which is just regular feminism with a case of the cutes.

We do not believe in postmodernism in any form, which is to say, we do not think the next great reformation of church history is going to be ushered in by a few Frenchmen with a bad case of brain snakes.

But of course, this "not believing" of ours must be incarnational. "Will you consider Cilvan College's prospective student week?" "Well, no. I actually wouldn't let my dog catch frisbees on the lawns of that campus." "Will you think about enrolling your daughter at Bleaton College?" "No, her mother and I are both in a twelve-step program for recovering evangelicals. We are at the third step, which involves toddlers and rudimentary musical instruments. I don't think you are ready for that yet." "Oh. What about a little donation then?" "Um, no." "Will you reconsider?" "No, I don't believe so."

CHAPTER 13

So Go Nomo to the Pomo

So in this little book I have written about the problems of postmodernism, what I have called the problem of European brain snakes. This might seem a little dismissive, but it all works out, because it actually is dismissive. Allow me to collect my thoughts on this brief epilogue.

First, postmodernism, and all the posturing and posing connected thereunto, is utterly inconsistent with the spirit of testimony that faithful Christians love to exhibit. Our testimony (*marturia*) is to the truth, and the truth is personal and ultimate. When I say the truth is ultimate, I do not mean ultimate in the concerns of our own little faith community. I mean Lord of all that is, Lord of Heaven and earth, and King of all nature. The truth is Jesus, and He is eternal life—and there is no other.

"And I fell at his feet to worship him. And he said unto me, See thou do it not: I am thy fellowservant, and of thy brethren that have the testimony of Jesus: worship God: for the testimony of Jesus is the spirit of prophecy" (Rev. 19:10). "He that believeth on the Son of God hath the witness in himself: he that believeth not God hath made him a liar; because he believeth not the record that God gave of his Son" (1 John 5:10). "I have not written unto you because ye know not the truth, but because ye know it, and that no lie is of the truth" (1 John 2:21). "But the anointing which ye have received of him abideth in you, and ye need not that any man teach you: but as the same anointing teacheth you of all things, and is truth, and is no lie, and even as it hath taught you, ye shall abide in him" (1 John 2:27). "This is he that came by water and blood, even Jesus Christ; not by water only, but by water and blood. And it is the Spirit that beareth witness, because the Spirit is truth" (1 John 5:6).

Anyone who can reconcile the aroma of these passages with the stench of postmodernism has already had too much graduate school, and should be sent home immediately.

This testimony is the basic reason why all postmodern pretense stands revealed for what it is—relativistic hash. But there are other criticisms that can be brought as well. The circus tent of postmodernism has no central pole, so there's that. But there are other observations that can and should be made.

The fact that postmodernists have offered cogent criticisms of the pretenses of modernism is neither here nor there—even though I grant they have done so. The reason it is neither here nor there is that modernists can offer cogent criticisms of the postmodernists as well. When two secular positions get to criticizing one another, they are often very astute in their observations, and many of their thrusts go home. After Ammon and Moab were done with Seir they turned on one another

(2 Chr. 20:23). Let them go to it, and then go get their stuff. But any Christian academic who in all seriousness publishes a series of papers on how Moab's post-structuralist critique is worthy of some more chin-stroking on our part is just acting like an Ammonite and should be sent to his tent.

Next, we should reject postmodernism because it isn't really postmodern. Before awarding the grand prefix *post* to anything, we should ascertain that it actually is describing something in the rear view mirror. If we look at the foundation stones of modernism, we should quickly identify one of them as being the thought of Darwin—evolution. But why is it that none of these johnnies are saying that they are post-Darwinian? Evolution is a metanarrative, but the only incredulity I can find anywhere is in the discussions of tourists in the parking lot of the Creation Museum. The postmodernists pretend that they are blowing up the foundations when they are actually just painting the eaves a different color.

And then, after we have rejected postmodernism because it is just the next stage of modernism, I will put forward the second half of my koan and say that we should reject it because it actually is postmodern. We should also reject postmodernism because, despite its strongest efforts to be an inconsistent parasite on the body of modernity, it remains a parasite that will in fact destroy its host. Modernity is not dead yet, but if this particular tapeworm has its way, that will eventually be accomplished, and the prefix post will come in fact to pass. Another foundational thinker for the modern project was John Stuart Mill, and the whole idea of liberty of thought. This is the basis for academic freedom and so on, but academic postmodernists are strangely drawn to the argument "because shut up." They have shown, they thought, that all orthodoxies are disguised power grabs, which actually turns out to be preeminently true of them. This is the basis for all the hate speech nonsense, and the absolute intolerance for any views other than their own. Someone has aptly said that progressives want diversity in everything . . . except opinions. This really is the result of postmodernism, and postmodernism really is post-freedom. That part is true enough.

And last, postmodernism has been defined as "incredulity toward all metanarratives," but the problem here is that this is not self-referential. Lack of self-awareness in this is the name of the game. "All metanarratives" is metanarratival, and far from displaying incredulity toward it, postmodernists are gulping it all down with the enthusiasm of a new JW recruit taking notes at a Watchtower conference. So let's not listen to them.

We should not be surprised at your inability to stand if your argument is that you have no legs.